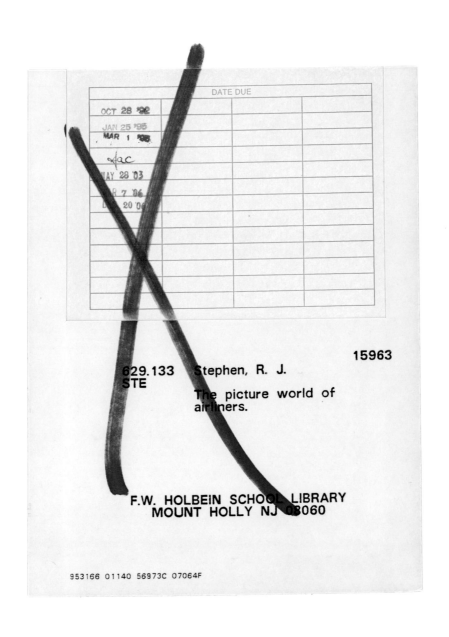

© 1989 Franklin Watts

First published in the USA by
Franklin Watts Inc
387 Park Avenue South
New York
NY 10016

US ISBN: 0-531-10724-8
Library of Congress Catalog
Card Number: 88-36275

Series Editor
Norman Barrett

Designed by
Edward Kinsey

Photographs by
Action Plus
Air France
Air New Zealand
Aviation Picture Library
British Aerospace
British Airways
Cathay Pacific Airways
Civil Aviation Authority
Delta Air Lines
KLM Royal Dutch Airlines
Scandinavian Airlines System
Thai Airways
Travel Press Service
Virgin Atlantic Airways

Technical Consultant
J. M. G. Gradidge

The Picture World of
Airliners

CONTENTS

Introduction	6
Aboard an airliner	8
The flight deck	10
Control and safety	12
Around the airport	15
Kinds of airliners	20
Facts	26
Glossary	28
Index	29

Airliners are the fastest way for people to get from place to place. They are not held up by oceans or mountain ranges. Airliners fly high above these natural obstacles that slow down other means of transportation.

△ Passengers board a DC-10 airliner. The doors of a big airliner are far off the ground. At some airports, movable staircases called jetways are used for boarding.

△ An airliner flies high above mountainous country, over land that is almost impossible to cross by any other means.

▷ Passengers sit in comfort and are looked after by stewards and stewardesses during a flight.

Aboard an airliner

A long-distance flight might last a whole day or a night. People eat and sleep on board. They watch movies and listen to music. There are special sections for kitchens and for toilets on big airliners.

▽ The cabin crew looks after the passengers' needs. They serve meals and provide cushions and blankets if required. They check safety belts and demonstrate other safety equipment.

△ Passengers traveling in first class have more room. Some airliners have sleeper seats for long trips.

▷ Some airliners have business class cabins. Business people are provided with special services to enable them to work and relax in comfort.

The flight deck

The pilots' cabin is called the flight deck or cockpit. Large airliners are flown by a crew of two or three – a captain and a first officer and sometimes a flight engineer.

The pilots' main concerns are when the plane is taking off and landing. In between, most of the flying is controlled by computer.

△ The captain sits on the left, with the first officer on the right.

▷ There are dials and instruments that show the plane's speed, direction and height and how the engines are running. On some planes a flight engineer sits behind the pilots.

Control and safety

At large international airports, there are takeoffs or landings every minute. All movements of aircraft on the ground or in the air are controlled from a tall building called the control tower.

Air traffic controllers tell pilots which taxiways and runways to use. They also guide planes approaching the airport or waiting to land.

▽ In many airports, the air traffic control rooms are housed at the top of a tall tower. The top control room is used for guiding planes on the ground. Operators in the lower one control planes in the air.

△ Air traffic controllers are in charge of several planes at once. They follow the movements of all planes above or approaching the airport on radar screens. If they don't do their work carefully, two planes might collide.

▷ Air traffic controllers talk to pilots by radio.

▽ A lesson in air traffic control.

◁ An inspector (right) with the captain of an airliner. Airliners and air crew receive regular inspections. All parts of an airliner's flying systems and body are also regularly checked. The engines, landing gear and other moving parts are carefully checked just before a new flight.

Around the airport

An international airport occupies a large area. Airliners need long runways for taking off and landing. A big jet requires as much as 4 km (2.5 miles) of runway. Planes often line up on taxiways before take off.

▽ Airliners move along a taxiway while waiting their turn to take off. Other airliners, big and small, can be seen around the terminal buildings loading and unloading passengers.

△ Ground staff loads baggage into the hold of a jumbo jet.

▷ An airliner is surrounded by service trucks as ground crews prepare it for a flight. Engineers check engine oil, tire pressures and other equipment. The plane is refueled, the cabins are cleaned and meals are loaded on board.

◁ A small passenger aircraft is checked by inspectors.

▽ Special airport fire trucks are always ready in case of an accident.

◁ Passengers hand their tickets in at the check-in desks. Their baggage is weighed and taken in.

▽ Passengers relax in comfortable lounges, waiting for their flights to be called.

The terminal buildings handle thousands of travelers every day. Passengers pass through check-in points, and passport, security and customs checks. The buildings contain stores, restaurants and lounges. Some modern airports have automatic trains for moving people between buildings.

▽ A hostess chats to young passengers in the departure lounge. Airlines make special arrangements for children traveling alone. They are escorted from the terminal building to the plane, where they are looked after by the cabin staff.

Kinds of airliners

Airliners vary in size. The latest Boeing 747s can carry 660 passengers. Small passenger craft are used for ferrying 5 to 10 people over short distances.

Airliners have two, three or four engines. The faster planes have jet engines. Aircraft with jet engines that drive propellers are called turboprops.

▽ The DC-10 is a big jet, powered by three engines.

◁ The Concorde is a supersonic jet. This means it travels faster than the speed of sound. It can cross the Atlantic Ocean from London to New York in about 3 hours, more than twice as fast as other jets.

▷ The Boeing 747 is the world's biggest airliner. It is sometimes known as a jumbo jet. It has two decks. Most of the passengers travel on the lower deck. The cockpit is on the small upper deck, where there are also seats for passengers traveling first class or business class.

◁ Passengers leave a Lockheed Tristar. The Tristar, or L-1011, is a medium- to long-range airliner that can carry as many as 400 passengers.

▽ A fleet of Boeing 737s. The 737 is used for short- and medium-range flights. It can carry nearly 150 passengers.

▷ The Boeing 727,
one of the most
popular of the
medium-sized jets.

Two short- to medium-
range airliners, an
Airbus A 300 (left) and
a McDonnell Douglas
DC 9 (below).

Some airliners are designed for short trips or for carrying a small number of people. These might be used as "feeder" planes between small and large airports.

Or they might carry business people from place to place. These executive planes are often run by companies for their private use.

▽ Jetstream 31s, twin-engined turboprop airliners. They are used for short trips or to feed main routes. They seat nearly 20 people.

△ The HS 125 is a business, or executive, jet. It seats from 8 to 14 passengers.

◁ A racehorse is led out of a small cargo liner. Airliners, big and small, are specially designed or adapted for carrying freight.

25

Fastest

The world's fastest airliner is Concorde. Its maximum cruising speed is 2,179 kp/h (1,354 mph). This is twice the speed of sound. Most other big and medium jets can reach speeds of 900–950 kp/h (560–590 mph).

Concorde's special shape is designed for speed. Its pointed nose has to be lowered for taking off and landing to give the pilot a clearer view of the runway.

△ Concorde, the world's fastest airliner.

Biggest

The Boeing 747 is the biggest airliner in more ways than one. It is the largest, widest and heaviest of all passenger airliners and can carry the most people. No wonder it is called the jumbo jet!

The body of a 747 is 70 m (230 ft) long. The wingspan, from wingtip to wingtip, of the largest 747s is 64 m (211 ft). With fuel tanks full, it weighs 395 tons, about twice as much as a Concorde.

The number of people that can be carried depends on the arrangement of the seats. The latest version of the jumbo jet, the 747-400, has a "stretched" upper deck and can carry 660.

Airliner "firsts"

The first airliners were made from bombers used in World War I, which ended in 1918. The first jet airliner came into service in 1952. It was the De Havilland Comet, and it could carry 36 passengers.

In 1959, Pan American World Airways introduced the first round-the-world service by jet airliners. The first aircraft on this service was a Boeing 707.

Flying boats

Flying boats, or seaplanes, have bodies that can float on water. They can take off from water and land on it. They are used mainly for small trips, often between islands. They carry only a few passengers.

△ A flying boat has floats to keep its wing tips out of the water..

More than just a wing

There is more in an airliner's wings than meets the eye. The wings contain the fuel tanks. They also have several surfaces that are moved by the pilot when taking off or landing. The pilot moves flaps out to increase the area of the wing.

Other flaps called ailerons

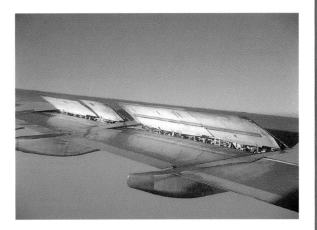

△ The spoilers are up as the pilot prepares to take the plane down.

are used for lifting one wing and dropping the other. The pilot uses these to turn the plane.

The spoilers are used to help the plane lose height faster. The pilot also uses the spoilers to help to slow the plane on the ground.

△ The spoilers are still up and the flaps are down as the plane touches down on the runway.

Glossary

Air traffic control
The department at an airport that controls all movements of planes, both on the ground and in the air.

Customs
The organization whose job it is to make sure that anything illegal, such as drugs and arms, is not transported over a country's borders. Passengers pass through customs at international airports. They pay a tax called duty on certain products bought abroad.

Feeder liner
A plane used to carry people from small airports to the major ones, where they can travel on main routes.

Flight deck
The cabin from which the pilots fly the plane. It contains all the controls and instruments.

Jet
A jet plane is one that has jet engines. The fuel (kerosene) is burned to produce the hot air that pushes the plane along.

Landing gear
The structure that carries the plane's wheels. It folds away into the plane's body or wing after takeoff.

Radar
A method used for keeping track of planes. Air traffic controllers can follow the movements of all aircraft in the area on their radar screens. Airliners also carry radar to spot storms or other aircraft.

Runway
The strip of concrete at an airport used for taking off and landing.

Supersonic
Greater than the speed of sound.

Taxiways
The roadways at an airport used by planes moving between the runway and the terminal buildings.

Turboprop
An aircraft with jet engines that drive propellers.

Index

ailerons 27
Airbus A 300 23
airport 6, 12, 13, 15, 19, 24
air traffic control 12, 13, 14, 28

baggage 18
Boeing 707 26
Boeing 727 23
Boeing 737 22
Boeing 747 20, 21, 26
business class 9, 21
business plane 24, 25

captain 10, 14
cargo liner 25
check-in desk 18, 19
cockpit 10, 21
Concorde 21, 26
control tower 12
crew 10, 14
customs 19, 28

DC-9 23
DC-10 6, 20
doors 6

engineers 10, 14, 20

feeder liner, plane 24, 28
fire truck 17
first class 9, 21
flaps 27
flight deck 10, 28
flying boat 27
fuel tanks 26, 27

ground staff 16

hold 16

inspector 14, 17

jet 15, 20, 21, 26, 28
Jetstream 31 24
jumbo jet 16, 21, 26

landing 10, 12, 15, 26, 27
landing gear 14, 28

meals 8, 16

passengers 8, 9, 15, 18, 19, 20, 21,
    22, 24, 25, 26, 27
pilot 10, 12, 13, 26, 27

radar 13, 28
radio 13
refueling 16
runway 12, 15, 26, 27, 28

safety 8, 12
security 19
sleeping 8, 9
speed 10, 26
spoilers 27
steward, stewardess 7
supersonic 21, 28

takeoff, taking off 10, 12, 15, 26,
    27
taxiway 12, 15, 28
Tristar 22
turboprop 20, 24, 28

wing, wingspan 26, 27